The Real-Life Adventures of Bobbie Sue and Her Sisters

BEA ROLLINS

Copyright © 2022 Bea Rollins
All rights reserved
First Edition

NEWMAN SPRINGS PUBLISHING
320 Broad Street
Red Bank, NJ 07701

First originally published by
Newman Springs Publishing 2022

ISBN 978-1-68498-681-1 (Paperback)
ISBN 978-1-68498-682-8 (Digital)

Printed in the United States of America

In memory of my mother, Lucille, my aunt, Carrie, and my sister, Zakiyyah, and also my sisters Blanche, Carrie, Frankie, and Brenda.

The First Day of School

I was happy. I was starting the first grade, and it was the first day of school. My mother, Louise, bought me a pretty blue dress to wear on the first day. Blue is my favorite color. Mom had pulled my hair up into a ponytail and tied it with a blue ribbon. I looked at myself in the mirror and was happy with the way that I looked.

I was going to be in Mrs. Parker's class as my two older sisters, Belinda and Gigi, had been.

They really liked Mrs. Parker because she was a family friend, a really nice person, and a wonderful teacher whose students really loved her. Mrs. Parker was my Aunt Cora's best friend, so I already knew her because she was at my aunt's house a lot. I lived with my Aunt Cora from the time that I was eleven months old until I turned six. I am from a family of eleven children, six girls and five boys. Aunt Cora helped by looking out for us. She kept an eye on us and made sure that we had something to eat.

I liked Mrs. Parker so much. She was always nice to me. She would bring me candy and play games with me. She would give me a hug and tell me that I was pretty. She always smiled a lot. I knew how kind she was, and I expected that I would be in her first-grade class as my two sisters had been. Both of my parents worked, so my sister, Gigi, had to take me to school on the first day. She was a year older than me.

Gigi was a prankster and liked to play tricks on me. When we got to school, she took me to Mrs. Gray's class instead of Mrs. Parker's class. She ran away, laughing, when she saw how scared I was. I had heard so many stories about how mean Mrs. Gray was to her students and how she kept a stick in her classroom to paddle her students with. I could not move. I just stood by her door and started to cry. Mrs. Gray heard me crying and came out of her classroom and tried to coax me inside. She kept asking what was wrong, and all I could do was cry. Although I was scared of the rumors about Mrs. Gray, she was very kind to me.

Finally, I heard another door open. It was Mrs. Parker, whose classroom was next door. She told Mrs. Gray that she would take me to her classroom. She took me by the hand, and I followed her into her classroom. Once inside Mrs. Parker's room, I was greeted with an array of learning and art stations. I went to the learning station first. I saw this little girl. She was very pretty, light brown-skinned with big brown eyes. Her hair fell to her shoulders in black curls. She had taken charge of the class and was bossing everyone around. I picked up one of the learning toys, and she took it from me and said that I couldn't play with it. I picked up a crayon, and she took it from me. Every time I picked up something, she would take it from me.

Finally, I had enough and went to the other side of the classroom, picked up a book, and started to read it. The little girl came over, gave me a toy, told me that her name was Bonnie Ray and asked me to play with her. I said, "Okay," and told her that my name was Bobbie Sue. We became best friends after that and played together every day for the rest of the school year.

The Train Ride

The first-grade teachers planned a field trip during the spring to Golden, a city two hours away from Johnsonville. My first-grade class had gone to the park and the creamery, but this trip was special because we were taking a train ride to Golden, and we would take a tour of the art museum. My sister, Gigi, received special permission to go on the trip with me. My Aunt Cora paid for both of us.

My class walked to the train station early in the morning. When the train rolled into the station, it was very loud with smoke coming out of the engine. My sister and I boarded the train and found seats. I decided to get up from my seat to go to the bathroom. I started to walk, and I could feel the train moving beneath my feet, and it scared me so much that I could not take another step, so I quickly sat back down for the rest of the ride.

When we got to Golden, there was a bus waiting to take us to the art museum. I enjoyed looking at all the pictures and had a good day at the museum. After we finished our tour of the museum, we went to a restaurant named Lucy's for lunch. We had a very good lunch of hamburgers, fries, and a cold glass of lemonade. After lunch, we all lined up to use the bathroom at the restaurant before we were taken back to the train station. During the train ride back, I stayed in my seat because of my fear.

The fear of that experience stayed with me, and I was terrified to ride the train after that. I avoided riding trains until my oldest daughter was four years old. I am no longer afraid, but if I stand up, and the train is moving, the fear comes back.

The Wedding

At the end of the school year, the first-grade teachers decided on doing a school play. It was called *The Million Dollar Wedding.* Zoe Smith was picked to be the bride, and Benjamin Henderson was picked to be the groom. The other boys and girls were all members of the wedding party and had to march in with their partners.

Mrs. Parker told me to tell my mother that I would need a long dress because I was going to be in a wedding for our school play. I told my mother what I needed, and she bought some yellow crepe paper and got on her sewing machine and made me a dress. Some teachers had used crepe paper in the past to make some dance costumes for the girls. That evening, when I got to the play, I was so embarrassed when I saw all of the other little girls with their beautiful, long, store-bought dresses.

Their mothers had curled their hair, and they all looked so pretty. I was embarrassed by my yellow crepe paper dress, and my hair was in a ponytail. I was afraid that the kids would laugh at me. I was in such shock that I don't remember marching in with my partner. My best friend, Bonnie Ray, was picked to sing a song to the bride and groom. The song was called "I Love You Truly."

She sounded so beautiful. She had a beautiful voice. Up until then, I didn't even know that she could sing. That's what kept my mind off how embarrassed I was to be the only little girl in the play who was wearing a yellow dress made out of crepe paper.

Two years later, I was in the third grade, and the third-grade teachers decided on doing *The Million Dollar Wedding* for the end of the school year. I told my Aunt Cora what I needed. Veronica Harris was picked to be the bride, and Matt Martin was picked to be groom. Aunt Cora bought me a beautiful long store-bought dress. It was blue and white, and I had white shoes and blue socks. She curled my hair and put blue and white ribbons in it.

When I got to the play, I saw all the other little boys and girls dressed in their finest. All the girls looked so pretty, and I felt beautiful as I walked down the aisle with my partner, like I did on the first day of first grade.

About the Author

Barbara Rollins was born and raised in Louisiana. She also lived in North Carolina and Michigan before settling with her husband in central California. Barbara is an avid reader who loved books as a child. She is a mother of three and spent their early years sharing her love of books and storytelling with them. As a result, her children are avid readers and book lovers too. This is the first book that Barbara Rollins has ever written.

CPSIA information can be obtained
at www.ICGtesting.com
Printed in the USA
BVHW011327040123
655461BV00027B/404